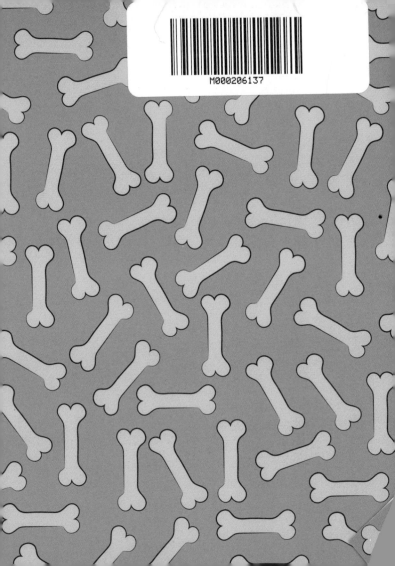

M000206137

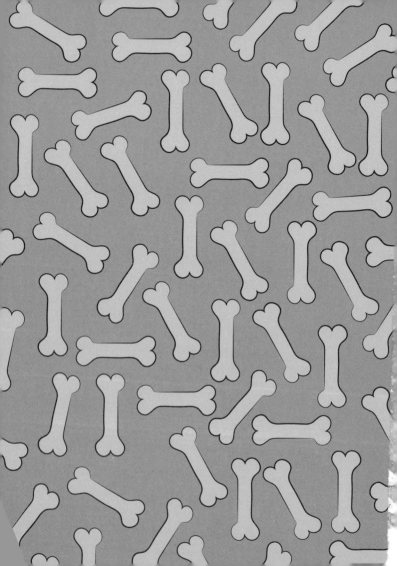

THE LITTLE BOOK OF
PAWSITIVITY

LIFE LESSONS
FROM DOGGOS

ROSIE PALMER

summersdale

THE LITTLE BOOK OF PAWSITIVITY

An Hachette UK Company
www.hachette.co.uk

Summersdale Publishers Ltd
Part of Octopus Publishing Group Limited
Carmelite House
50 Victoria Embankment
LONDON
EC4Y 0DZ
UK

www.summersdale.com

Printed and bound in China

ISBN: 978-1-80007-343-2

DEDICATED

TO MY FAMILY

JEREMY, ANGELA, JACK, WILL AND STAN THE HOT DAWG

And in loving memory of my grandma, Maria, whose Lhasa Apso, Dougal, brought her untold happiness

INS-PAW-ATION

The inspiration behind this book is Stan, a very scruffy but loyal sausage dog. Stan is a miniature wire-haired dachshund who embodies every pawsitive trait we associate with dogs: unconditional love, energy, loyalty, respect, humour and openness.

Stan's pawsitive qualities have gained him a loyal social media following. He is a mood-boosting "dogfluencer" who uses his pawsitivity to remind his human following that there is always a reason to smile. Stan (@StanTheHotDawg) has over 80,000 Instagram followers and over 18 million video views. Stan's unrivalled bushy brows, dapper beard and puppy-dog eyes charm his loyal following around the globe. When Stan wears his tweed coat, his followers call him "Sherlock Bones".

Highlights of Stan's career include Lionel Richie re-posting a video of him raising his paw to his hit "Hello" and the renowned social media account, We Rate Dogs, giving Stan a score of 12 out of 10.

CONTENTS

WELCOME

INTRODUCTION

Dogs! They're universally adored by us. They show us unconditional love. As soon as they sense we're sad, they will make it their life's mission to make us smile. Unlike humans, we connect with every dog instantly; they look at every one of us with sparkles in their eyes and show us boundless affection and unwavering pawsitivity.

Someone put it accurately when they said, "Everyone thinks they have the best dog, and none of them are wrong." This book is a playful tribute to every dog who has ever lived and a reminder to their much-loved humans that pawsitivity conquers all.

CHAPTER ONE

LIFE LESSONS FROM PAWESOME BREEDS

Every dog breed has its own
quirky personality traits we
can learn from.

BASSET HOUNDS TEACH US

SOMETIMES
YOU NEED
A LAZY
DAY

FRENCHIES TEACH US

WRINKLES ARE JUST SMILE LINES

CORGIS TEACH US

IF YOU'VE GOT IT, FLAUNT IT

I LIKE
BIG
MUTTS &
I CANINE
LIE

DACHSHUNDS TEACH US

YOUR
DIFFERENCE
IS YOUR
STRENGTH

BULLDOGS TEACH US

EMBRACE
YOUR RESTING
GRUMPY
FACE

CHIHUAHUAS TEACH US

NOT TO TAKE
OURSELVES
TOO
SERIOUSLY

DOGGOS TEACH US

DIVERSITY BREEDS SUCCESS

CHAPTER TWO

DOGGO MANTRAS

Doggos understand that the
key to happiness is simple:
to eat well, play well, love
well and sleep well.

Here are some of their wise
mantras that will give us
a new lease of life!

PAWSITIVE VIBES ONLY

WHEN YOU HAVE A STRUGGLE, HAVE A SNUGGLE

LIFE CAN BE RUFF BUT WE TOUGH

HARD WORK PAWS OFF

STAN & UNCLE WILL

EYEING UP A DRUMSTICK

SLEEPY STAN

PLAY TIME!

STAN THE HOT DAWG

STAN THE HOT DAWG

CHAPTER THREE

STAN'S
HAPPINESS
HACKS

Stan always wakes up with a
wag in his tail and a spring in
his lil' step. These are Stan's
top tips to remind us there's
always a reason to smile.

SPEND TIME WITH THE PEOPLE YOU LOVE

STAN & UNCLE WILL

SLEEPY STAN

ALWAYS PRIORITIZE SLEEP

NEVER LOSE SIGHT OF YOUR DREAMS

EYEING UP A DRUMSTICK

PLAY TIME!

NEVER HIDE YOUR ENTHUSIASM

CHAPTER FOUR

PAWS & RELAX: DOGGO SELF-CARE INSPIRATION

Na-mutts-ste!

Our relentlessly pawsitive best friends
who don't waste time worrying are
the best source of inspo, and remind
us to be kind to ourselves.

NAP
LIKE IT'S
YOUR
JOB

LIVE IN THE MOMENT

FIND JOY IN THE SIMPLE THINGS

DOWNWARD DOG IS ALWAYS A GOOD IDEA

Su-paw-stars

DOUG THE PUG

ENDAL

JOE THE JOCK

MARNIE THE DOG

WENDY

SU-PAW-STARS

CHAPTER FIVE

INSPIRING CANINE TAILS

These inspiring dogs
teach us to never give up, to
support each other through
the good and the bad times,
and to approach any
challenge with courage
and pawsitivity.

I SHIH-TZU YOU NOT

Marnie's story was the ultimate canine rags-to-riches tail. Originally known as Stinky, she lived on the streets, sick and almost blind, before being taken into a shelter. After being adopted by her new dog mom Shirley Braha, she travelled to New York City by train and stunk up the entire carriage ☹. Safe and sound in her furever home, her vision improved, and her confidence grew. However, other medical conditions meant her head was tilted permanently, and her unusually long tongue stuck out.

These quirks are part of Marnie's charm. When her dog mom set up an Instagram, Marnie gained millions of followers and she soon began hanging out with celebrities like Katy Perry, Selena Gomez and Demi Lovato. Not too bad for a street dog originally called Stinky!

MARNIE THE DOG

WENDY

YOU'VE GOT A FUR-IEND IN ME

When Hunter Van Brocklin was ten, he learned to walk again after major surgery with the help of Wendy, his beloved dog. Wendy is a gentle giant: a black Great Dane with white-tipped paws. Hunter was diagnosed with cerebral palsy at the age of two, and had struggled to walk without assistance, but Wendy helps him enjoy his passion for long walks. Hunter gives her directions by pulling on her harness and Wendy helps Hunter by maintaining his balance.

Hunter's mom, Kelly, says that their bond brings her to tears, "It is so pure and true. She protects him everywhere they go. It's like having an extra parent around, she doesn't take her eyes off him." Hunter and Wendy have grown up together and have formed an inseparable bond. Hunter said, "One day, I'll climb Mount Everest with Wendy. She'll always be there for me."

HOLY
PUGAMOLE

What can be achieved in a lil pug's life, you may ask? Well... Doug might surprise you and remind you that anything is pawssible! Doug the Pug is a celebrity doggo, with millions of followers on social media and billions of views on Facebook. He has also appeared in music videos for Katy Perry, Fall Out Boy and DNCE. The Mayor of Nashville, Tennessee even named 20th May "Doug the Pug Day".

Doug's mission has "always been to make people smile each and every day". As a result, Doug and his dog mom set up the Doug the Pug Foundation. Doug regularly visits children with cancer and other life-threatening diseases to bring some puggy love during tough times. The foundation also raises money to contribute to their treatment.

DOUG THE PUG

ENDAL

THE ULTI-MUTT SUP-PAWT

Endal the lab dedicated his life to helping his owner, Allen Parton, a veteran of the British Royal Navy. After suffering injuries whilst serving in the Gulf War, Allen looked to Endal for support. Endal's abilities were extraordinary: he learnt to press buttons, understand sign language commands, use switches, load and empty a washing machine, retrieve items from supermarket shelves, use ATM machines and was even able to return his owner's card to his wallet. Endal also saved his owner's life when Allen was knocked out of his wheelchair by a car. Endal managed to put Allen in the recovery position, covered him in a blanket, barked for help, and even found his lost mobile phone.

Endal is quite simply a su-paw-star. He was recognized with the canine equivalent of the Victoria Cross for gallantry and devotion to duty and was named the "Dog of the Millennium" by *Dogs Today* magazine. Thanks fur everything you did to help Allen, Endal.

SIZE DOESN'T MUTT-ER

This is like a modern-day David and Goliath. But this time the battle was between Joe, a tiny 2.7 kg Yorkshire terrier from New Jersey in the US and a near 200 kg black bear.

Joe was keeping his dog mom, Deborah Epstein, company whilst she was recovering from a car accident. Deborah suddenly heard Joe barking like crazy and then saw a towering black bear coming into her house. Her feisty Yorkie wasn't impressed by the large uninvited guest and when the bear went for his food, Joe had clearly had enough. "The bear was heading for his food dish bowl, and you don't touch Joe's food dish bowl. And he actually got the bear to turn around and chased him out the door."

Deborah said: "I saved him from the pound, and he saved me from a bear... We're even."

JOE THE JOCK

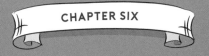

CHAPTER SIX

DOG
MEMES

The two greatest things that
dogs provide us with are
love and laughter.

These relatable dog memes
reflect that. They will either
warm your heart or make you
howl with laughter.

BE THE PERSON YOUR DOG THINKS YOU ARE

A LITTLE KINDNESS GOES A LONG WAY

SHOUT-OUT TO MY DOG FOR EATING THE SAME MEAL EVERY DAY & NEVER COMPLAINING

THEY SAY THE

BEST

THERAPISTS
ARE FURRY
WITH FOUR LEGS

I WORK HARD SO I CAN SPOIL MY DOG

DOGS
LEAVE
PAW PRINTS
ON OUR
HEARTS

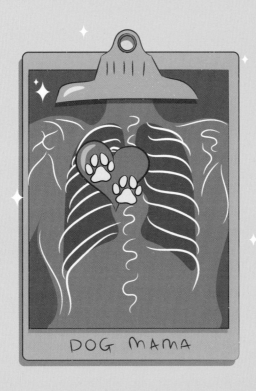

DOG MAMA

DOGS HAVE BEEN
A HUMAN'S
BEST FRIEND
FOR OVER
30,000 YEARS

CHAPTER SEVEN

THE ULTI-MUTT DOG FACTS

Doggos have been a human's best friend for over 30,000 years, so there's no wonder we're fascinated to learn more about our furry companions. I've fetched together some of my favourite facts that will make you realize why they're so pup-ular.

THE QUEEN IS THOUGHT TO HAVE TAKEN HER CORGI SUSAN ON HER HONEYMOON

IN THE BEATLES' CLASSIC, "A DAY IN THE LIFE", A SOUND WAS ADDED THAT ONLY DOGS CAN HEAR

WHEN YOU STARE INTO A DOG'S EYES, YOUR BRAIN RELEASES LOVE AND HAPPINESS HORMONES

STROKING A DOG ACTIVELY LOWERS YOUR BLOOD PRESSURE

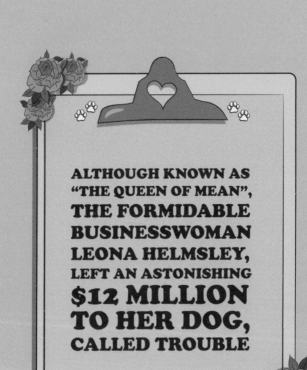

ALTHOUGH KNOWN AS "THE QUEEN OF MEAN", THE FORMIDABLE BUSINESSWOMAN LEONA HELMSLEY, LEFT AN ASTONISHING $12 MILLION TO HER DOG, CALLED TROUBLE

CHAPTER EIGHT

DOG ZODIACS

Have you ever wondered what
dog breed you're most similar to?
Thought so!

Each breed has been matched with
the personality traits associated
with specific star signs so you can
judge your canine compatibility.

ARIES:
COURAGEOUS & FRIENDLY

TAURUS:
EXTRAVAGANT & SASSY

GEMINI:
ENTERTAINING AND UNIQUE

CANCER:
LOYAL, CARING
& OCCASIONALLY MOODY

LEO:
BIG-HEARTED, A NATURAL LEADER & GENEROUS

VIRGO:
GOOD IN A CRISIS, HUMBLE AND AN OVERTHINKER

LIBRA:
EXTROVERTED, GOOFY AND CHARMING

SCORPIO:
LOYAL, SELF-ASSURED AND RESPECTFUL

CAPRICORN

Dachshund

SAGITTARIUS

Bichon Frise

SAGITTARIUS:
INDEPENDENT, SASSY AND ADVENTUROUS

CAPRICORN:
AMBITIOUS, STUBBORN BUT LOVING

AQUARIUS:
OPTIMISTIC, ENTHUSIASTIC
AND ACTIVE
PISCES:
EMOTIONALLY INTELLIGENT
AND EMPATHETIC

@ROSIEAPALMER

ABOUT THE AUTHOR

ROSIE

Rosie is a writer, designer and illustrator, but most impawtantly a passionate dog lover.

Rosie's life changed overnight when she became "dog mom" to Stan the Hot Dawg. Stan showed her unconditional love and companionship. Stan has taught her the importance of pawsitivity, completely changing her outlook and inspiring her to create this book to spread "Pawsitivity" across the globe.

STAY
PAWSITIVE

Have you enjoyed this book?
If so, find us on Facebook at
Summersdale Publishers, on Twitter
at **@Summersdale** and on Instagram
at **@summersdalebooks** and get in touch.
We'd love to hear from you!

www.summersdale.com

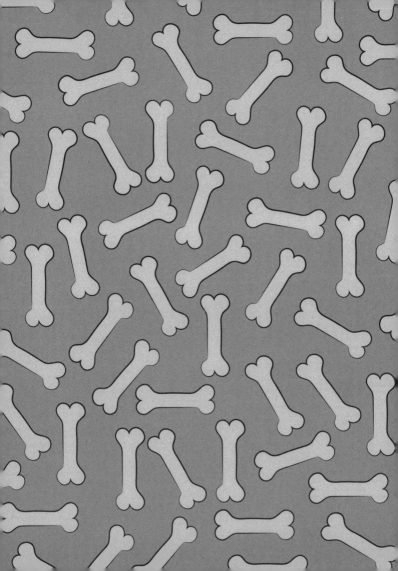

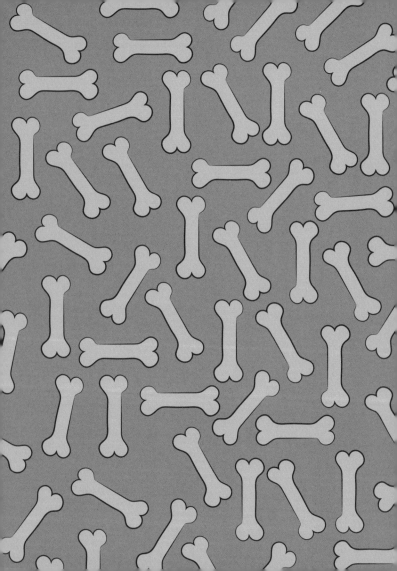